WORDS RAIN DOWN

A Journey in Poems

written by:
Muminah Muhammad

To order additional copies of this book, contact:
Xlibris
844-714-8691
www.Xlibris.com
Orders@Xlibris.com

ISBN: Softcover   978-1-6698-3871-5
       EBook   978-1-6698-3870-8

Print information available on the last page

Rev. date: 07/21/2022

Table of Contents

Words Rain Down

I feel words rain down
Lifting me up
Wholeness all around
Of Inspiration breathing me
Seeing me
Letting me feel my being
As I am reeling
From stinging words and comments
Those that are Heaven sent
Reach me
Teach me
Healing is a gift
That erases the rift
Healing is my gift
To others I uplift

Journey

Journey up to a higher stream
Careening down a hill
Down stairs
Starting and stopping
Feeling no fear
I have a vehicle
A 2 wheeled bicycle
Allah uplift me
Allah uplift me
Uplift me Allah
I find myself praying
As I speed toward
An unknown destination
As I awake
I find I was praying
In my dream
I find my consciousness
Has upgraded to a higher stream

Break Free

I've tried and tried to suppress it for so long
Trying to tell myself daily that the timing is all wrong
And after being pushed too deep too far
I've created a raging internal war
One day my Inner Creativity
Breached the contract of my naivety
Hot torrents of nourishing lava explode
Releasing years of delicious overload
Covering my burning lies
With a fiery flaming rise
Of my Inner Phoenix from the ashes
Dousing the reason for my hot flashes
My authentic artistic truth has forged it own track
And forever it will surge on fueled by flashbacks
And memories that go clickety-clack clickety-clack
And healthy applause of my delicious comeback

Am I Waiting

Am I waiting for my life to come to me
Unbottled emotions exploding from me
I speak I talk I monologue
From years of experience of a halfway dialogue
Not sure what's in front of me
Transforming inside like alchemy
Changing negativity to positivity
I lack the foresight to know the future
Right now the present is the treasure
The past the key
To opening my heart; my spirit; my soul; my mind and my body
I laugh, cry and sigh
I laugh, cry and sigh
I shout, laugh, cry and sigh
And furtively I search the hidden corners of the intersectional circles inside
Cavity of soul opening wide

One Day

One day I won't doubt what I'm thinking, feeling hearing, or seeing
One day when something bad happens I won't go reeling
One day I won't have to go to sleep early
One day I won't miss Fajr if I go to sleep late
One day I won't miss any salaats at all when I'm angry at Allah
One day I will forgive me for any and everything
One day I will realize that I am not responsible for someone else's anger, frustration, sadness or pain
One day my shoulders won't tense when someone says something uncomfortable, mean or intense
One day I will know when those One days are
One day will be the day

Spirit

Fire in my spirit
Peace in my soul
Thoughts cool and whole
My body feeling peace
I am a woman, who has lots of goals
I am working on this piece
To put in my first book
Words Rain Down
Listen to my poem
About the stuff I'm made from
From way up above
To down below
My experiences have made me, gifted spiritually
Now I'm trying to equip myself, physically
Allah is the one I worship at least five times daily
I'd like to find a way to write about my life
The ease and the strife
The boring and the interesting
And the things that make my heart sing
'Cause there's Fire in my Spirit
Peace in my soul
Emotions running even
Thoughts cool and whole
My body feels how this poem ends
P E A C E

Running

I see you hiding there
Running from I don't know where
Come and talk to me
I don't charge it's free
We'll talk together
So you don't feel so under the weather
I have dreams and hopes and mystery
Goals and wishes and history
What is your story
No need to cry
Or wonder why
Smack down shame
It's so lame
You're not alone
Put down your phone
I'm here for you
Where there was one now we are two
I see you hiding there
Running from, I don't know where

Flying

Fly high
Fly low
It doesn't matter where you go
Dream big
Dream small
Just dream and hope and wish and plan
About all that you can
See your future like a TV screen
Soon you will be living in that scene
Allah allows
The seed you sew
To grow
Now you know
Believe in your truth
Be like a sleuth
Find the clues to joy and power
And make your life into a well foundationed tower
Straight to heaven one day
Stopping at a lot of stops along the way

She

She sits
She flits
She flows
She goes
She comes with news of my future life
Telling me to be prepared to be a wife
Don't worry about the strife
Laughing and joking she smiles at me
And reminds me delicately
That the winter months are for hibernating ideas
To nurture my heart
To begin to start
And in spring let my ideas grow
Let them flow
Smile and believe
That will relieve
Any anxiety about failure
And help me look to the future
Instead of fearing
The hibernation season nearing

Death

When death happens
People are all around
Memories abound
Sometimes things are left unsaid
Sometimes we wish we were kinder
We wonder when we'll be happier
Friends or family even associates matter
Death takes your feelings and makes them flatter
When death creeps around
Nonchalantly
No apology
When death happens
People are all around
Tons of memories abound

Angels

Neither male
Nor female
Neither male
Nor female
They simply are
Some that fly, Some that stand Some that sit
Some that speak in silence and With their wings flit
Bringing a message
What do we envisage
Neither male nor female
They simply are
Alive
So take a dive
In light
What is light
But Love, Joy and brightness in sight

Too Early

It's too early in the morning
For me to think of problems
Your problems
My problems
It's too early in the morning
For me to stay awake
And too early to go to bed
The sun is up
The birds are singing
Grab me my coffee
Pass me my tea
It's too early in the morning
For me to do much but wake up

Tender and Sweet

It grows between us
Tender and sweet
Brings us closer together
Tender and sweet
Swirls around us like angels in Salat
Tender and sweet
Like a new book opened
Tender and sweet
Like a box of chocolates
Tender and sweet
His voice
Tender and sweet
My laughter
Tender and sweet
Our love
Tender and sweet

Moments

We are no more
Our similarities
Have turned to differences
Where we once calmed each other
Now we fight or sit in cold silence
We have gone our separate ways
And left behind
Sadness
Madnes
And discordant memories
Of if only you
If only I
What if
And it just wasn't meant to be
We are no more
But in my softest moments I wish we were

Fear

Fear is that creepy crawly knotty dread feeling
That makes you feel as if something is stealing
Your very reason for being
Sweat erupts in icy droplets that shine
At your forehead and stink under your arms
That stomach hardening gut wrenching feeling
That tightens your throat so your raspy breathing
Then stand your hairs on end
Makes the atheist pray :
God just help me out of this, I swear I'll believe again
As it snakes into your psyche
Shorting out logic and truth to pull out all roots of reality
Allowing the reeds of horrid fantasy
To play with your panic buttons
And create a nightmare that paints its mark on you
Fear is that totally unknown irrational consequence
That reminds you to have Faith in an equally unknown Benevolence

Rage

Lava rips through my veins
Hot explosions pound my heart
Irrational lightning flashes logic apart
Raging fires cause burning pains
Turning Emotions like Hurricanes
Pants my breathing
Violent rhetoric taunts my reasoning
Thick gray smoke looming
Thunder loud voices booming
I be Mad
I are Angry
I be Furious
I am Raging
Inside my soul, blue flames crackle cackle and spit higher
Probing my spirit to reach up and Aspire
Beyond the fear of loss
To Find a Smoky Faith
That Steams me to toss always old beliefs and peel new truth from old lies
Dissipating anger wafts into the swatting away of big black ants and tiny white flies

Racism

Global white supremacy
This reality which I never knew
For 3 years racism struck my eyes
It crushed me
I know that it is a trial many face
I grieve I was told I had equity
Then as an adult had it stolen from me
Nobody told me that I had to carve equity for myself
Nobody told me that I would be considered less because of my face
Nobody told me that I was considered a lesser human race
Because of caramel brown skin
Nobody told me that not everybody believes Black is beautiful
Beautiful and great
Racism : it gave me the gift of a destiny

Destiny

Nobody told me that I would not be considered Mi'k Maq because my skin is caramel brown
I was given a gift to teach the world about Equity
I need to challenge that Blackness is Evil
The good thing is I had 29 years to see only the great Black. . .
I can teach that greatness to the world with Ihsan
I will live a long life because there is so much ignorance
Ihsan to teach the gift of seeing Allah in everything and everyone
Equity is a manifestation of this great gift of Ihsan
The world desires equity
Hidden beneath veils of ignorance always lies the craving for truth
Once I was crushed by racism
But only for one violent year
I grieved and now I am uplifted with a Destiny
To teach a clarity of truth

Proud

To all who want to live the truth from the inside
There is one way to know pride
Tell the secrets deep inside
Don't let the secrets burn
Or make your guts churn
Let the hurt you hold so tight go
Allow your life to flow
Let your presence be
Gain the prize of being free
Befriend sadness
Kiss the lips of madness
Hold hands with fear
Hug joy and bring it near
In all the time you hope for
In all the dreams you yearn for
Something shouts from deep within you
Let it out and embrace it too
From high above to way down deep
To truly be able to win
You must love yourself to the outside starting from within

Ramadan

This is a poem about Ramadan
I am a woman who has to go through Ramadan without fasting
Many people cannot fast in Ramadan so they have to pay for people to eat every day
I am a woman who has to go through Ramadan without fasting
What is Ramadan without fasting it is blessing it is prayers it is
Qur'an it is names of Allah it is it is it is Ramadan
I am a woman who has to go through Ramadan without fasting
And I call upon a God greater than myself greater than anything I have
ever known greater than any imagination I have ever had
To bless me to forgive me to have mercy upon me
And true reward for any little and individual deed
And this month I am a woman who has to go through Ramadan without fasting
How is your Ramadan

Echo Echo

She told me she could hear herself in conversation
How informative what an education
She can hear her own voice
Double talk by Allah's choice
Echo Echo
Echo Echo
It's the workings of her mind
She sometimes uses music to unwind
Other times she sits in her thoughts
Is it a miracle, a disorder or evolution
She is amazing she doesn't need a solution

Belief

A wise barn owl stands
Rare enough not to be seen in other lands
Brown and red and beautiful
Looking for its next meal
Prey that will make her feel
Like her stomach is full
Her feathers shine
She is a sign
Of belief and prayer
So lovely and rare
A wise barn owl

Conscious

1000 thoughts float through my mind
Do you hear that
Nothing
What do I feel
The beginning of life
Conscious creativity
The movement before the stillness before the silence
I listen for it
I find myself listening for sound
Then relaxing into stillness
A long pause
A goodbye
A hello
The absence of thought
Alert
Conscious
Still
Being

Dreams

In dreams we are taken away to another place far away from here
What do you dream of
I dream of trees in summer and sunny days
snow rarely falls in my dreams
When I am inside, I feel warm environs and that I'm always welcome in brightly lit surroundings
A few times I have been in the third universe, 4th universe even the 5th
universe talking to one of the wisest men who ever walked
Today I was scooted away to another dimension where frightening and
powerful creations, that looked so ordinary scared me
Dreams take us away, far away even though we are right here

Walking In My Dreams

I am always walking in my dreams
I am always walking in my dreams
In sun and snow and by streams
Under trees, by the road walking
Walking in my dreams
Walking by the beach
Walking, the ground within reach
Cars driving by
Planes flying in the sky
Walking down paths with and without landmarks
I'm always walking in my dreams
Then one day I was on a bicycle in my dreams
Tell me what does that mean

Circle of Dreams

We sit
For a bit
On a lighted circle floor
No walls and no doors
Up in the 5th universe
Surrounded by black silky space
Telling me of Love
Telling me of Peace
Reminding me of Deen
Teaching me the Unseen
Of flowers and blooms
Of the future and visions
So I just don't watch televisions
New moons
And full moons
Waves and a beach
Smooth talking
Smooth talking
And Holy dreams alive

Emily

She smiled
And lit up the world
She wore her hair straight not curled
A little clumsy at dancing
Often took risks Brave and chancing
Intelligent and funny
Kind and her spirit sunny
I love my friend so sorry she's gone
But in my heart she lives on

Poetry Flowetry

Poetry
Flowetry
Go with me
Sew with me
Seeds of hope
Seeds of power
Seeds of tomorrow
Poetry
Flowetry
Go with me
To another world while staying right here
No need to stress, no need to fear
I take you to worlds of expertise
Rhymes that put your heart at ease
Another day another dollar
With my words there's no need to hollar
Poetry
Flowetry
Go with me
Sew with me
A new you
While the old you
Stays completely intact
Come on will attract
Poetry
Flowetry
So come on go with me

Communication

C-C-C Communication is my new station
Dropping words on a page brings me elation
They can be healing or ammunition
Telling stories about things that have gone right
Dropping essays and rhymes like They're outta sight
I can tell you right now it feels so right
Words and videos are a tool for the lockdown
Who says this time is to be without sound
Music and dance and laughter though I'm homebound
I will stay well
I won't let this be hell
I'll have stories to tell
Lockdowns aren't fun
They're like a gun
But one day it will be done
And when the lockdown ends
We can again be with family and friends
And words on a page is what inspiration sends
C-C-C-Communication
Dropping words on a page brings me elation
They can be healing or ammunition

Introducing Me

I am me
I love me
I understand me
I appreciate me
I allow me to be me
I give permission for me to be me
I am happy to be me
I am on a never ending journey of being me
I am me
I love me

Free

Free from the pain and agony your words and actions cause me
I am free
Free to be the person I choose to be
I am now the owner of me
I am free
I have my own values thoughts and beliefs
No more emotional blackmail for me
I have become strong enough to be me
I am free

Healing

Flashes of thought go through my mind
Negative experiences on rewind
How do I heal
What is real
Emotional overload
I'm trying to decode
The mental flip flops
Physically I'm tip top
I pause for a minute
And I just sit
Chapters and verses come to the surface
And I go forward instead of regress
I move to a place of tranquility, calm and peace
And all praise due to God, ease
Praise be to God after every hardship is ease

Still Waters Run Deep

Still waters run deep
Like a road uphill that's so steep
Sometimes my heart is so broken I fear it will never end
Other times there is so much joy I feel I have enough to lend
How is it that my soul can hold so much emotion
Waves of feeling that have tides like an ocean
I think
I feel
I do
I am
I BE
A woman full of mystery
Quicksilver Gemini thoughts that transform like alchemy
A complex simplicity
Of still waters running so deep
Still waters run deep
So much so, that when the damns of compartmentalised resistance breaks
There is a gushing flow of spiritual life
That makes my heart cool and deep like a lake

Printed in the United States
by Baker & Taylor Publisher Services